Chamber Music for Two String Instruments

by Samuel Applebaum
edited by Mary Wortreich

FOREWORD

To the Teacher:

This Chamber Music book is to be started when the pupil reaches page 5 of the Samuel Applebaum String Method. However, it can be used in conjunction with any good string method.

It can be played by:

Two Violins — Two Violas — Two Cellos — Two Basses.
Violin and Viola — Violin and Cello — Violin and Bass.
Viola and Cello — Viola and Bass — Cello and Bass.

To the Pupil:

To derive the greatest enjoyment from playing chamber music, you will want to train yourself to do the following:

1. **To Sight Read.** You must memorize the sensation of reading ahead. In this way you will be widening your peripheral vision. Play one measure—look away—and try to play as many notes as you can in the next measure. Practice this regularly to improve your sight reading.

2. **To Develop a Beautiful Tone.** Avoid touching two strings. If you do, move your right elbow a bit higher, or lower, to find the right string level.

If you scratch on any note you may be pressing the bow on the string a bit too firmly. Try drawing the bow a bit faster and playing a bit lighter.

To develop the best possible quality, experiment by drawing the bow in the center between the bridge and the fingerboard, or by drawing the bow closer to the fingerboard, or to the bridge. There is only one lane on which to draw the most beautiful tone, depending, of course, on how loudly you are playing and how quickly you are drawing the bow.

3. **To Develop Tone Color.** Practice playing loudly and playing softly. You might practice this with scales or with lines in this chamber music book. You must also learn to play gradually louder, and gradually softer.

Learn how to accent certain notes by applying a bit more pressure and by drawing the bow a bit faster at the start of the note.

4. **To Play Musically.** Try to find out where each phrase begins and ends. Does it begin on an up beat or does it start on the beginning of a measure? Does it start in the middle of a measure? Many times you will allow a slight pause (or breath) before you start the new phrase.

To play musically, you will play the last note of many phrases a bit softer than the previous note.

Listen carefully to your partner. If you have the melody, play just a bit firmer. If your partner has the melody, play a bit softer. However, when both parts move together in thirds, sixths or in octaves, the dynamic level should be the same.

When both parts move together, try to use the same amount of bow.

5. **To Play In Tune.** Listen very carefully to each other. When you practice alone, compare as many notes as possible to the open strings. If the note is out of tune, move your finger higher or lower until it is in the correct spot on the fingerboard. Memorize just what you did to play the note in tune.

EACH BOOK IS COMPLETE IN ITSELF, BUT ALL ARE CORRELATED WITH EACH OTHER.

The CELLO Method
For Class Instruction
or
Individual Tutoring

EACH BOOK CAN BE USED SEPARATELY. HOWEVER, ~ ~ *WELL-BALANCED* ~~EDULE~~ RY ED ITH ELF.

ETUDES FOR TECHNIC AND MUSICIANSHIP	CHAMBER MUSIC FOR TWO STRING INSTRUMENTS	CHAMBER MUSIC FOR STRING ORCHESTRA	THREE SEPARATE CELLO SOLOS WITH PIANO ACCOMPANIMENT
Interesting Etudes which are designed to develop a fine left hand and a well-poised bow arm, as well as the fundamental principles of good musicianship. The object is to correlate technic-building with musicianship.	A collection of beautiful duets for any two string instruments which are interchangeable. Excellent for chamber music performance. Optional piano accompaniments are available in separate publication.	A collection of lovely chamber music works which may be played by string orchestra or string quartet, or various other combinations of string instruments, with piano accompaniment.	For concert use, but correlated to the Method, transcribed by Samuel Applebaum. 1. *Petit Valse Brillante* . . . . .Benoni Lagye 2. *Valse Blvette* J. B. Duvernoy 3. *Three German Dances* . . . . .L. van Beethoven

1. Spring Dance

Moderato (Key of G) "𝄐" means a slight pause with the bow remaining on the string.

18TH CENTURY

2. The Clock

"+" means left hand pizzicato.

Allegretto (Key of C)

TRADITIONAL

3. Ländler

When the 2nd of two repeated notes is the 1st note of the next measure, we usually accent that note. We also make a slight crescendo to that note. "s" means to play the note a bit softer. "〻" means to lift the bow before starting the next note.

GERMAN FOLK DANCE

4. Aria

18TH CENTURY

5. Two German Dances

18TH CENTURY

6. Country Dance

Allegretto (Key of G) "s" means to play that note softer. Observe the dynamic marks.

ITALIAN FOLK SONG

7. Air

Allegretto (Key of F)

G. P. TELEMANN

(Melody)

6

8. Two Minuets

I Allegretto (Key of C)

18TH CENTURY

II Moderato (Key of D)

9. Bouree

Allegretto (Key of G)

G. SAMMARTINI

10. A Courtly Dance

J. B. LOEILLET

Moderato (Key of D)

EL 2382

11. Swiss Dance

Allegretto (Key of D)

LOUIS MARCHAND

12. Cotillon

Moderato (Key of B♭)

HENRY BATON

f - 1st time
p - 2nd time

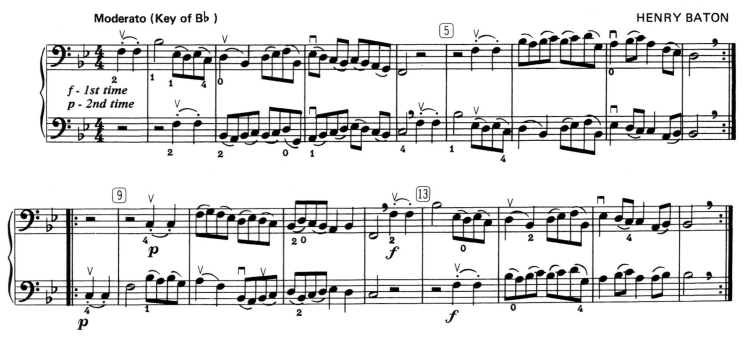

13. An Episode

14. Air and Minuet

EL 2382

15. Allegro

With life (Key of G)

J. M. LE CLAIR

16. Siciliano

17. Contre Dance

18. Sarabande

Moderato (Key of F)

J. B. LOILLET DE GANT

19. Scherzo

Allegro (Key of C)

CZECH TRADITIONAL

EL 2382

20. Prelude

FROHLICH-HOHMANN

Allegretto (Key of D)

(Melody)

21. Rondo

Allegretto (Key of G)

JAMES HOOK

22. Gavotte

Andante (Key of G)

J. AUBERT

23. Minuet

W. A. MOZART

24. Bouree

HENRY PURCELL